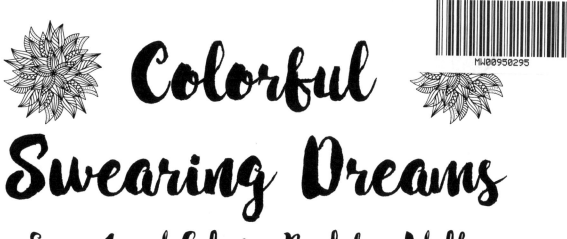

Colorful Swearing Dreams
Swear Word Coloring Book for Adults

IS YOUR STRESS LEVEL HIGH?
DO YOU WANT TO SWEAR OUT LOUD
TO LEVEL IT DOWN?
THIS BOOK WILL KICK YOUR STRESS AWAY!

Multiple studies revealed that coloring mandalas, geometric patterns & other shapes helps reduce stress and anxiety for adults.

This swear word coloring book will allow you to enter in a relaxed state by focusing in what you are doing and blocking out the nonstop thinking or other distractions. Those swear word designs will make you laugh and relieve your stress by expelling your negative thoughts.

This book contains 20 pages of beautiful & intricate designs mixing up with funny swear words that will connect with you.
Each page is single-sided for getting the best coloring experience.

TIME TO COLOR THE STRESS AWAY!

MW00950295

Colorful Swearing Dreams

Swear Word Coloring Book for Adults

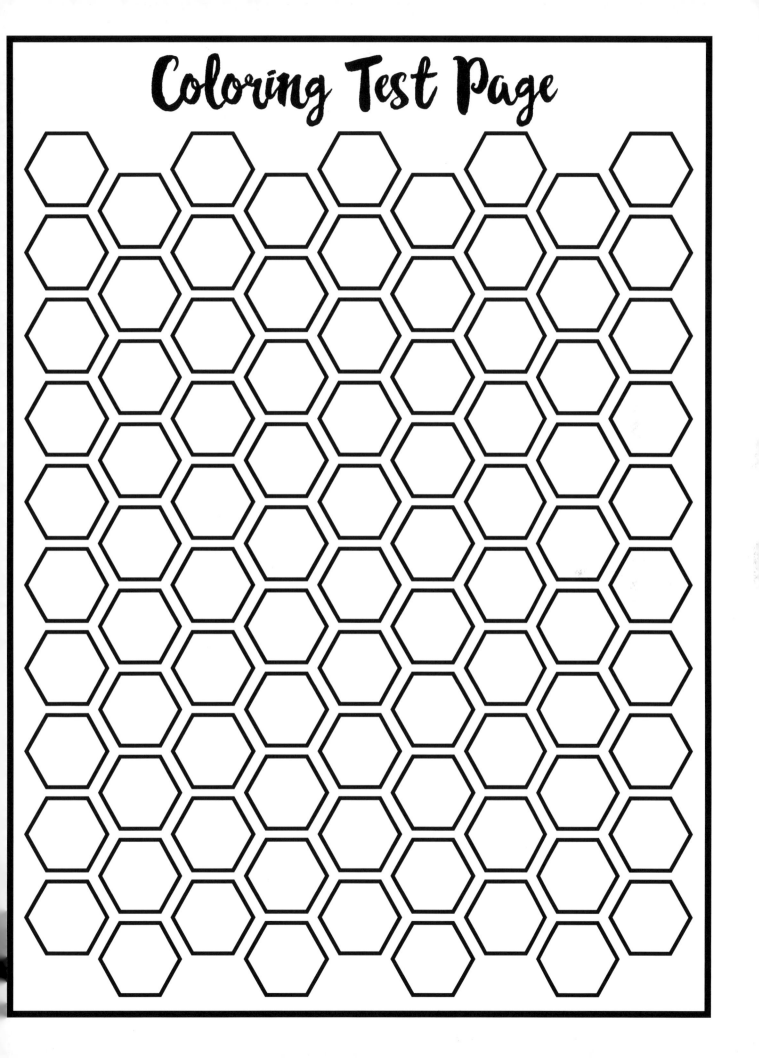

Coloring Test Page

Colorful Swearing Dreams

Swear Word Coloring Book for Adults

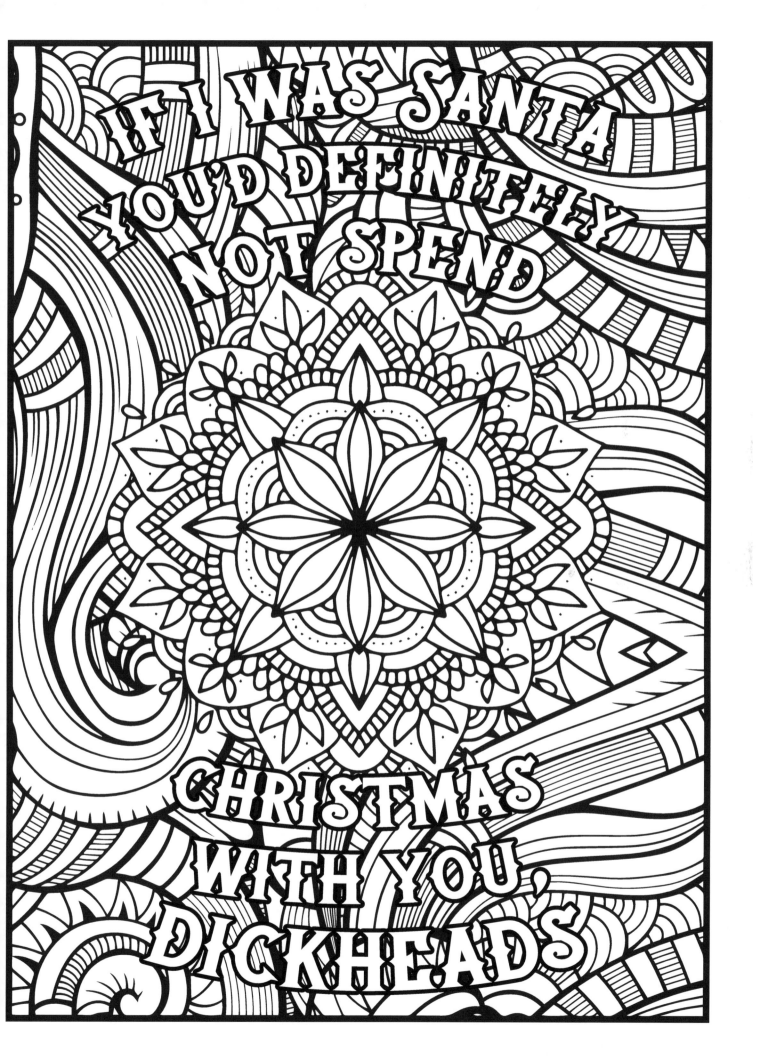

Colorful Swearing Dreams

Swear Word Coloring Book for Adults

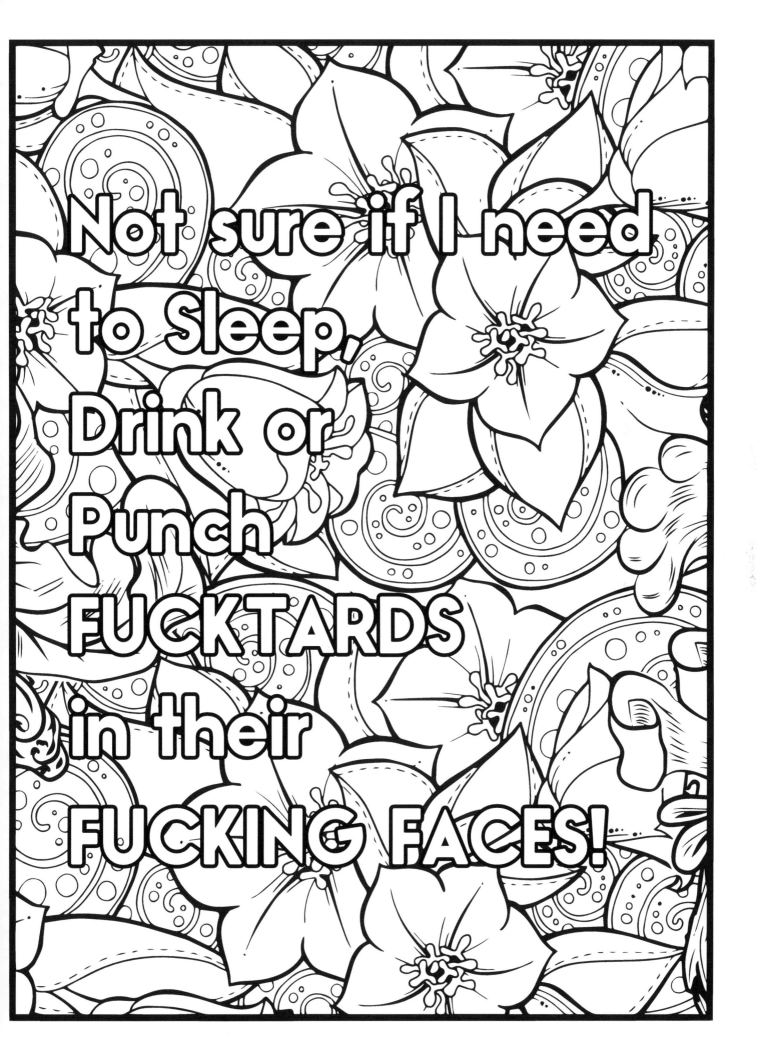

Colorful Swearing Dreams

Swear Word Coloring Book for Adults

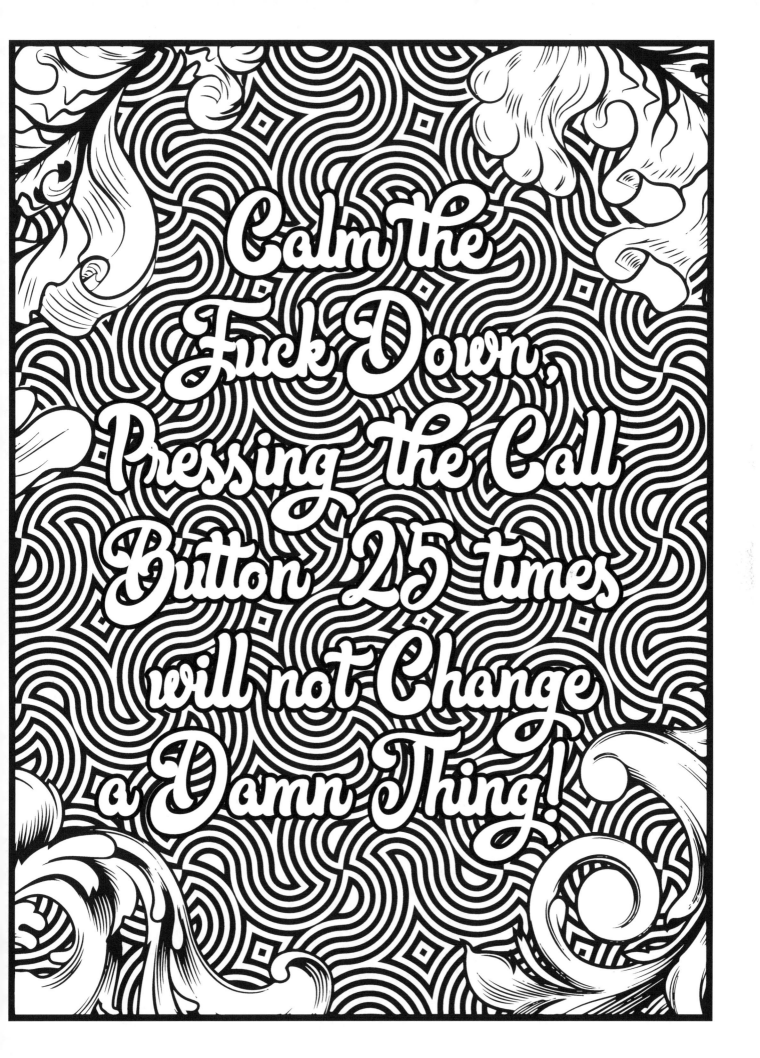

Colorful Swearing Dreams

Swear Word Coloring Book for Adults

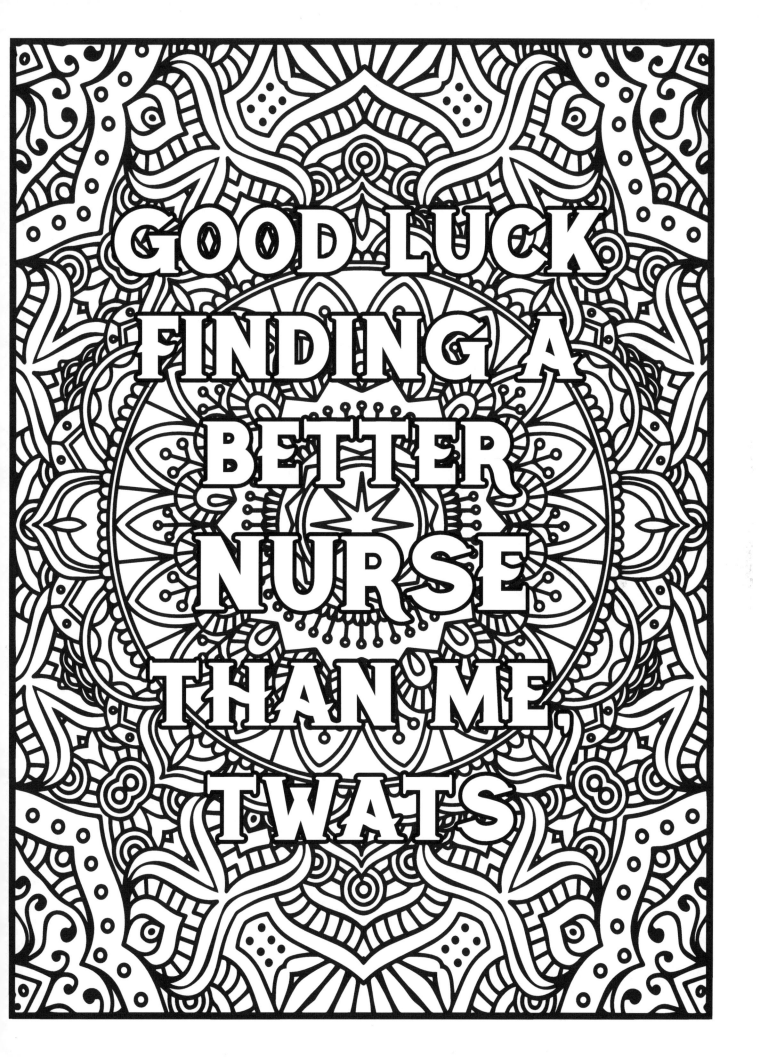

Colorful Swearing Dreams

Swear Word Coloring Book for Adults

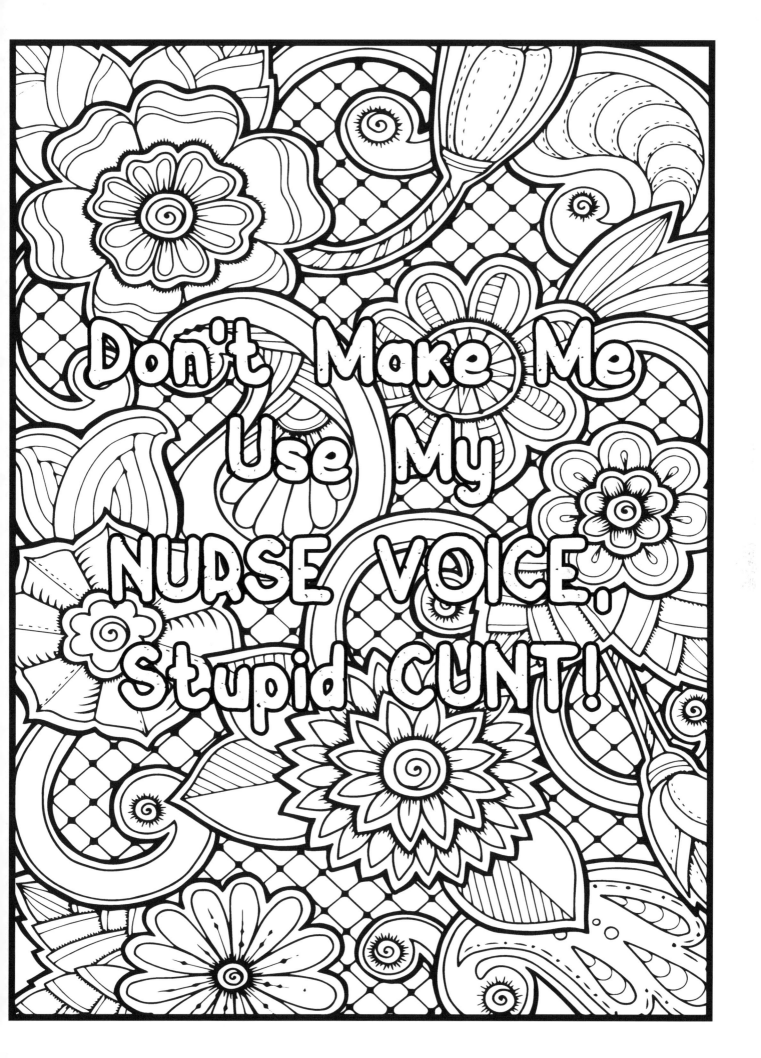

Colorful Swearing Dreams

Swear Word Coloring Book for Adults

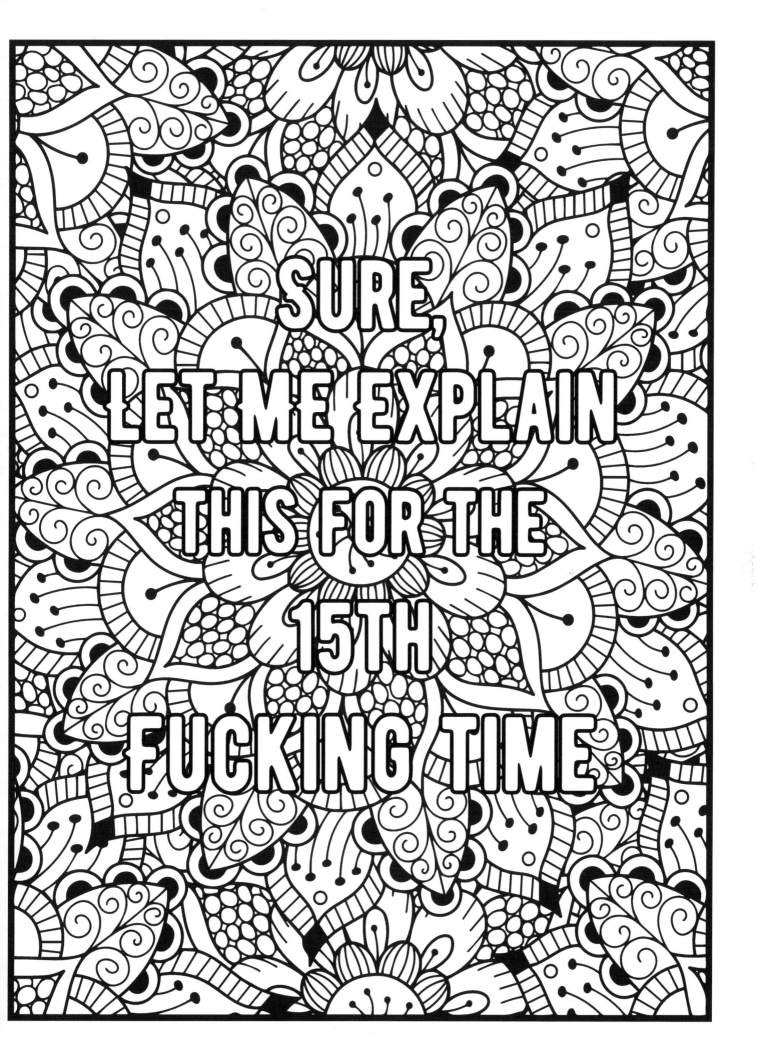

Colorful Swearing Dreams

Swear Word Coloring Book for Adults

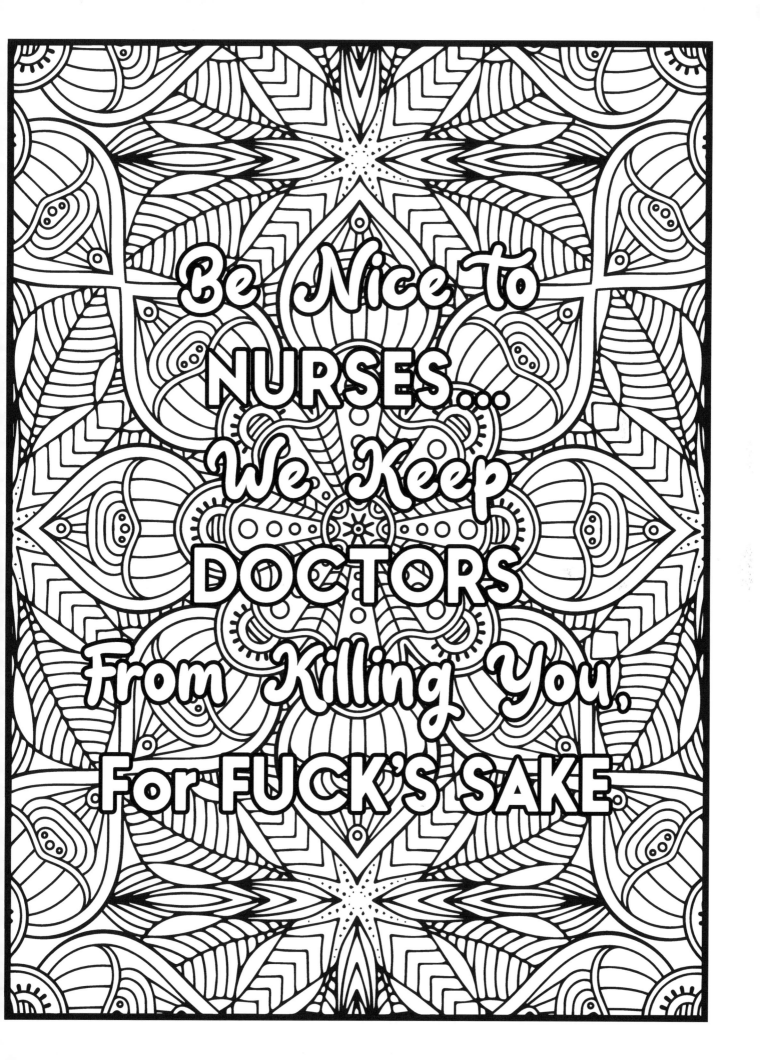

Colorful Swearing Dreams

Swear Word Coloring Book for Adults

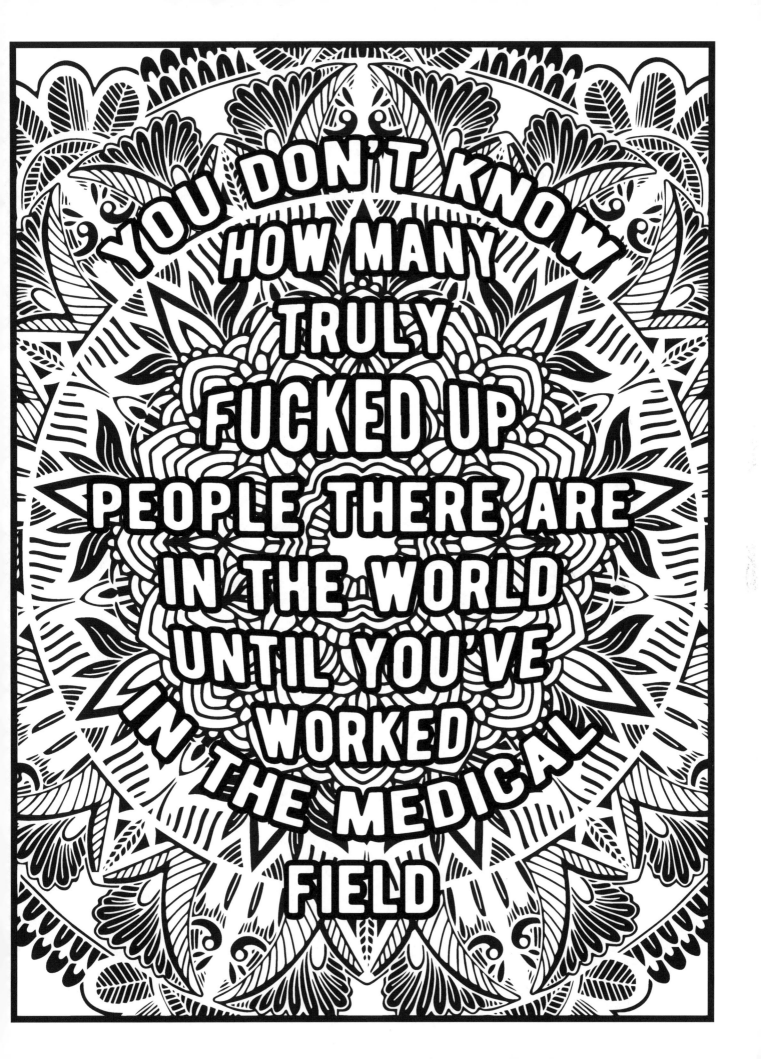

Colorful Swearing Dreams

Swear Word Coloring Book for Adults

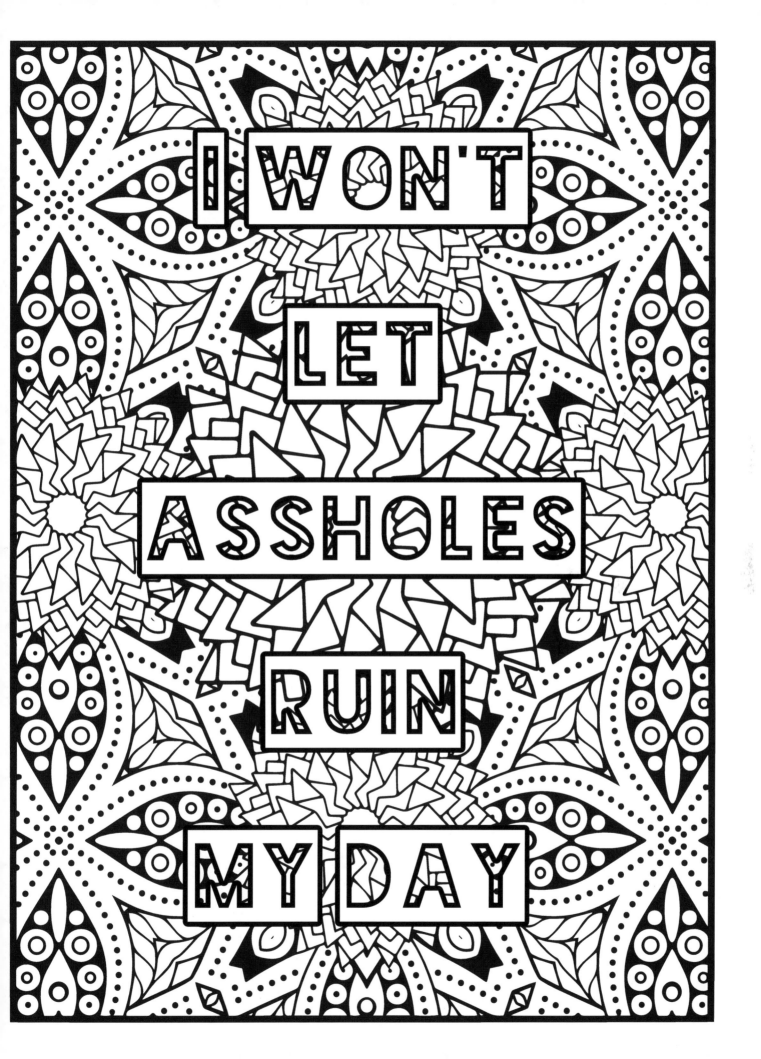

Colorful Swearing Dreams

Swear Word Coloring Book for Adults

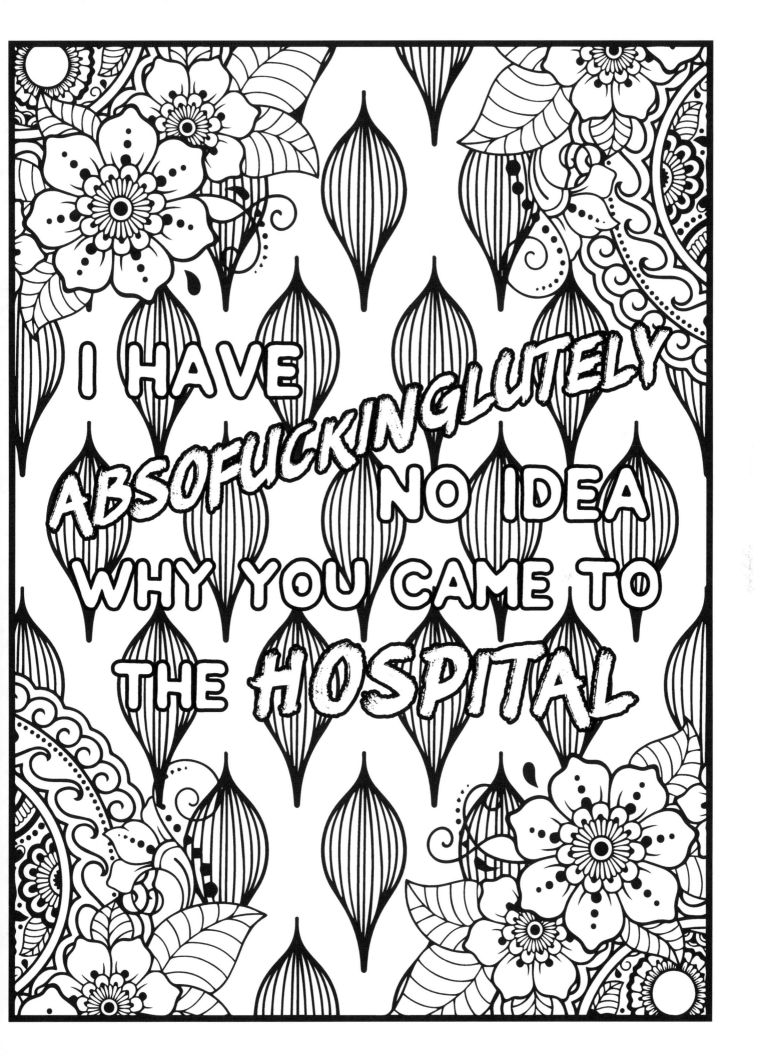

Colorful
Swearing Dreams

Swear Word Coloring Book for Adults

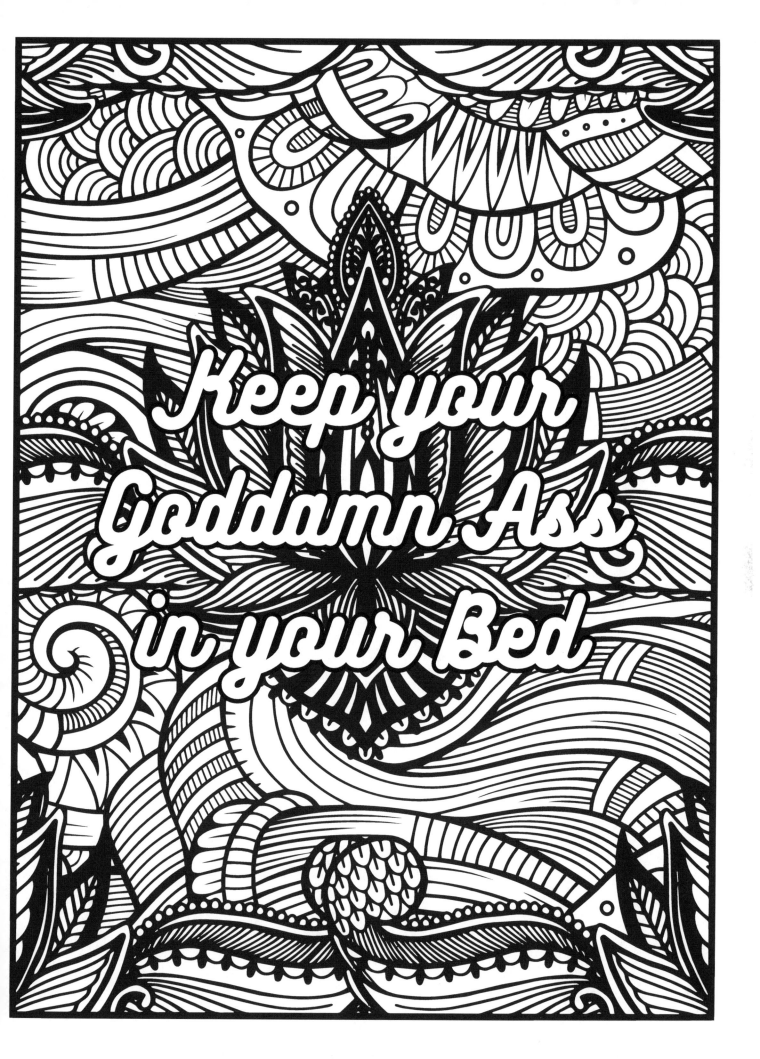

Colorful Swearing Dreams

Swear Word Coloring Book for Adults

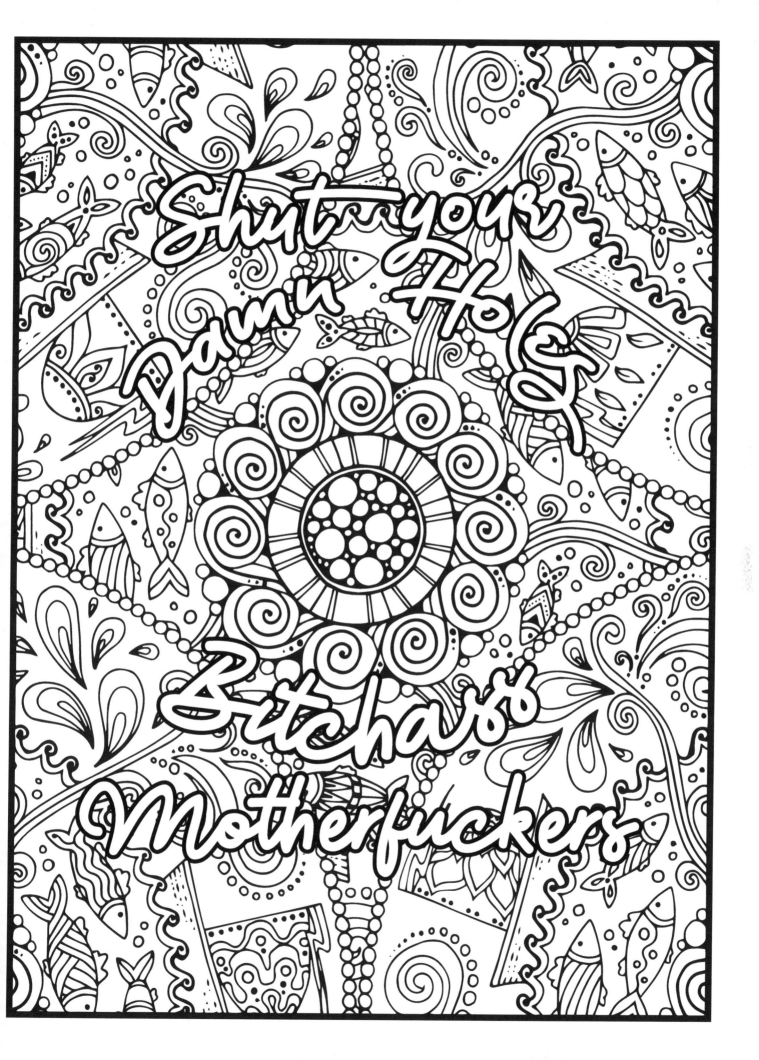

Colorful
Swearing Dreams
Swear Word Coloring Book for Adults

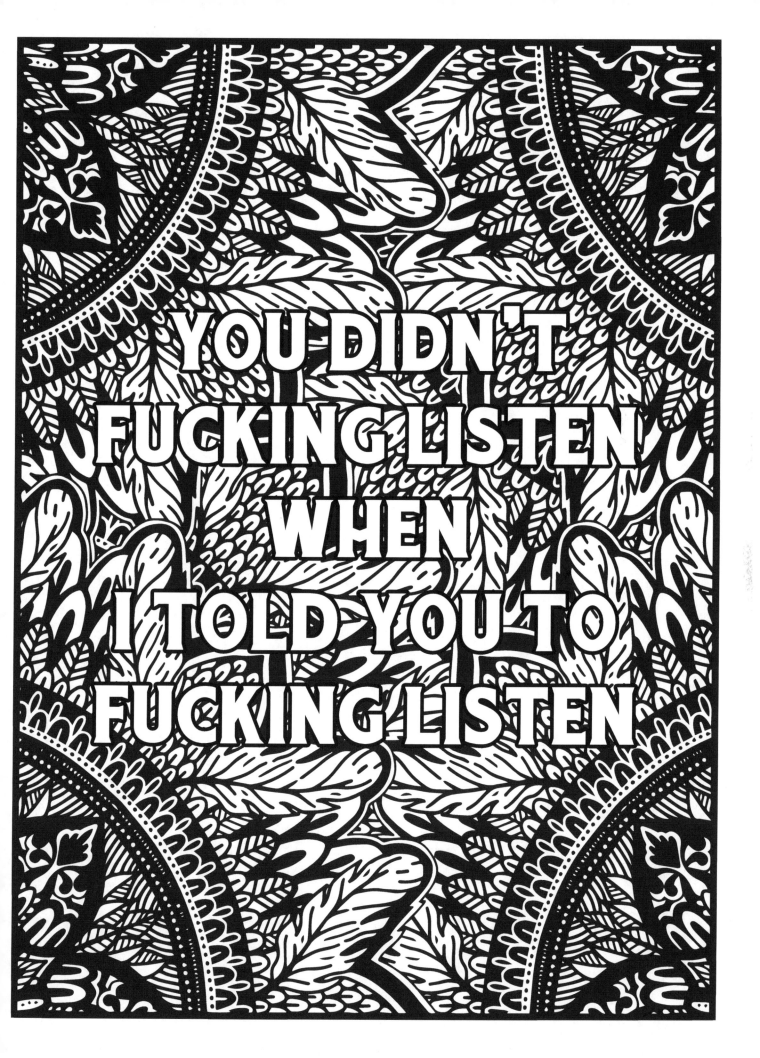

Colorful

Swearing Dreams

Swear Word Coloring Book for Adults

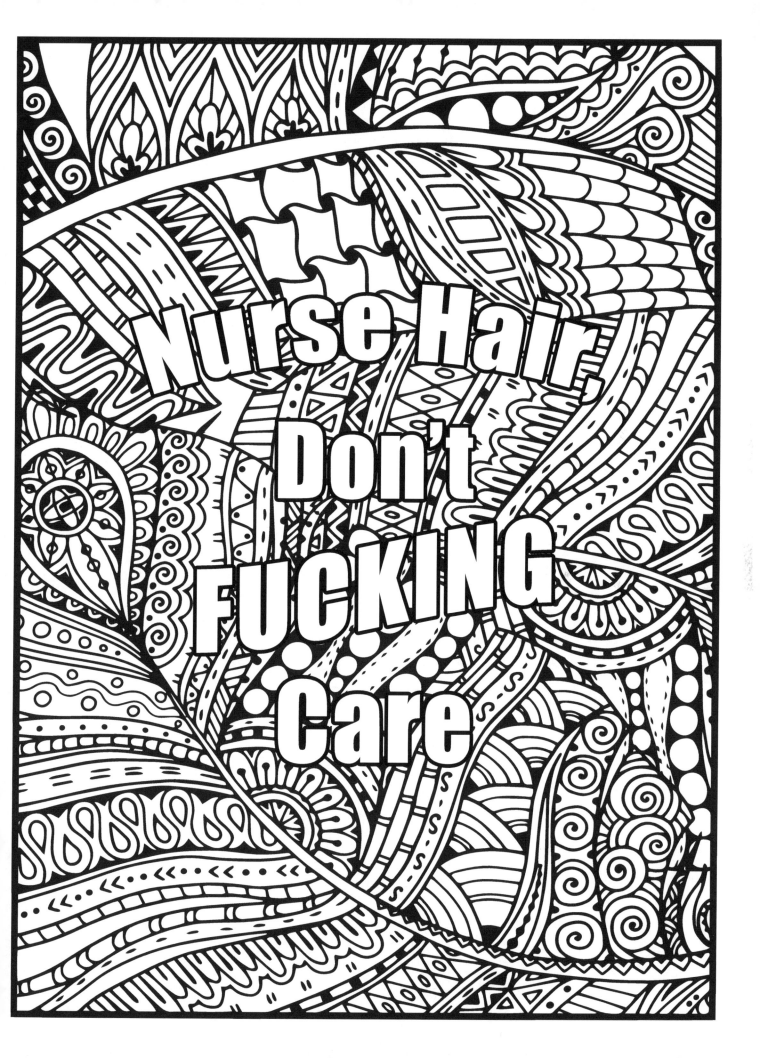

Colorful Swearing Dreams

Swear Word Coloring Book for Adults

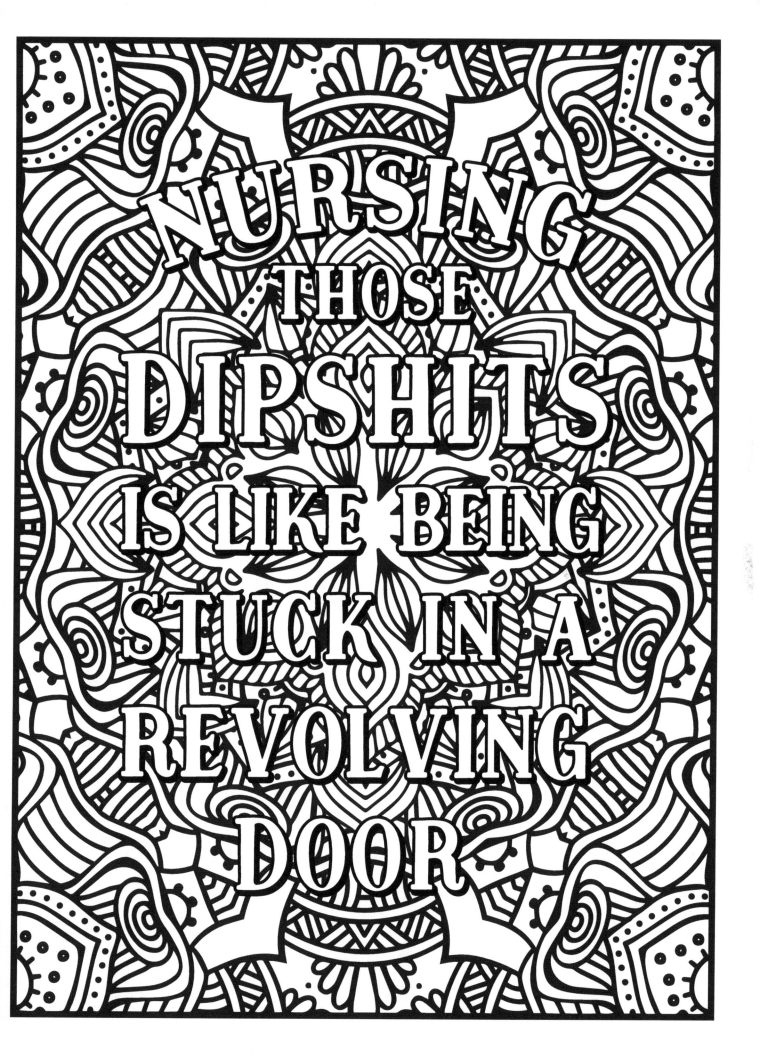

Colorful
Swearing Dreams

Swear Word Coloring Book for Adults

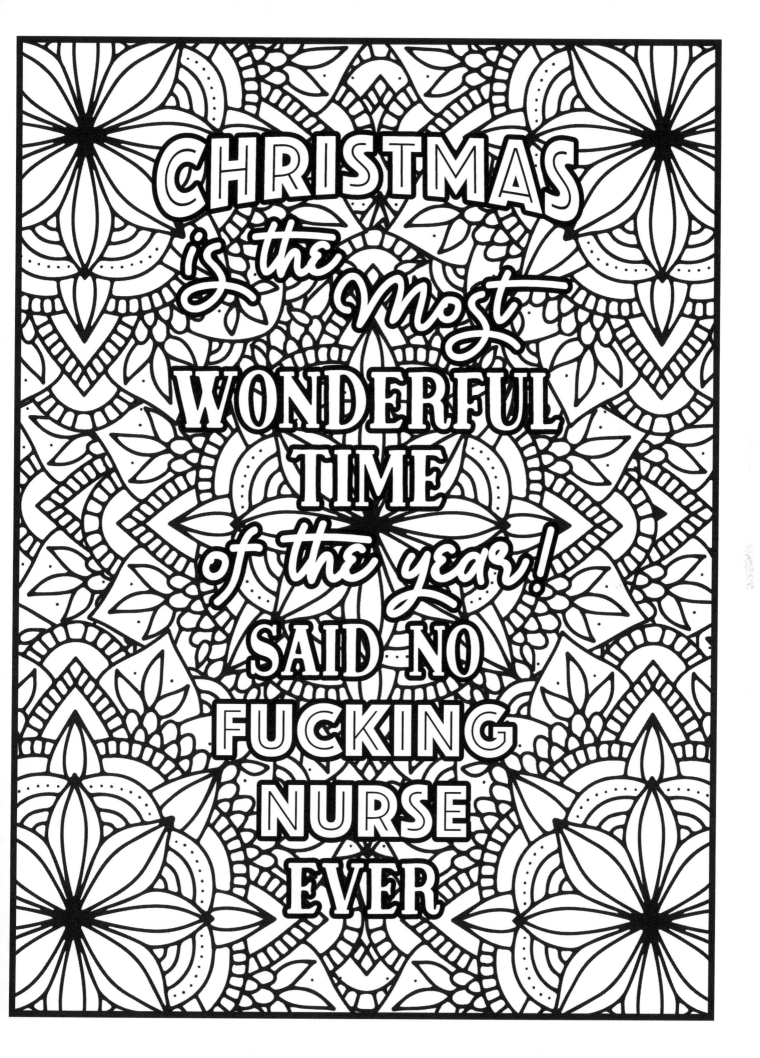

Colorful Swearing Dreams

Swear Word Coloring Book for Adults

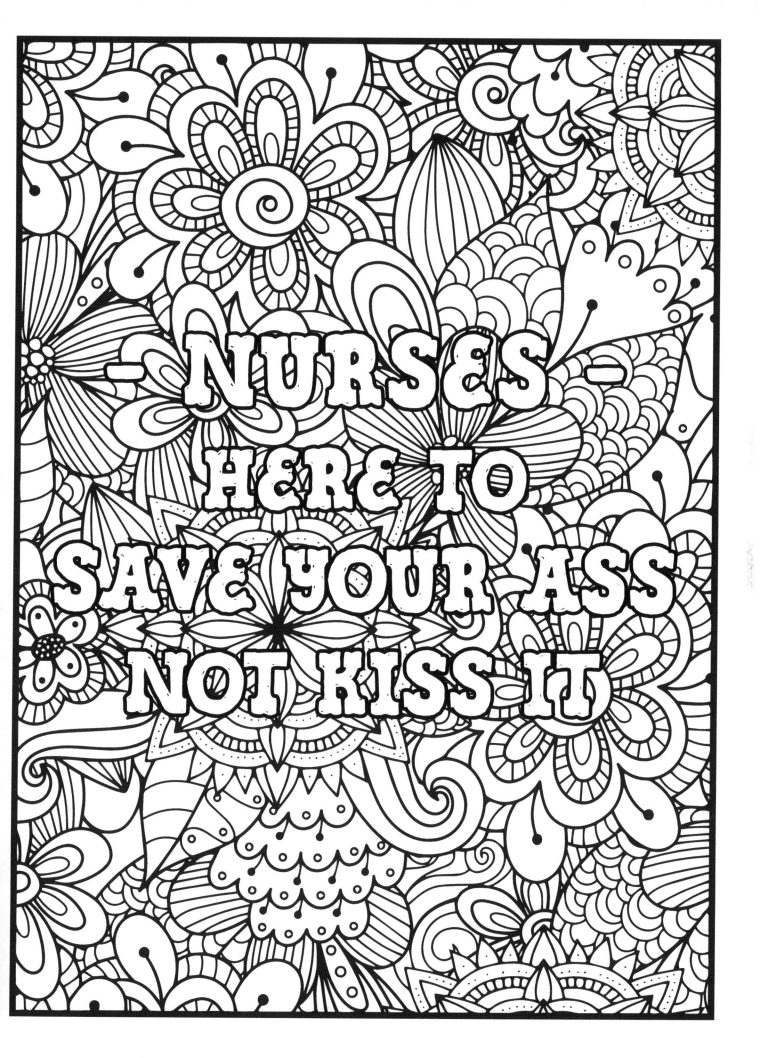

Colorful Swearing Dreams

Swear Word Coloring Book for Adults

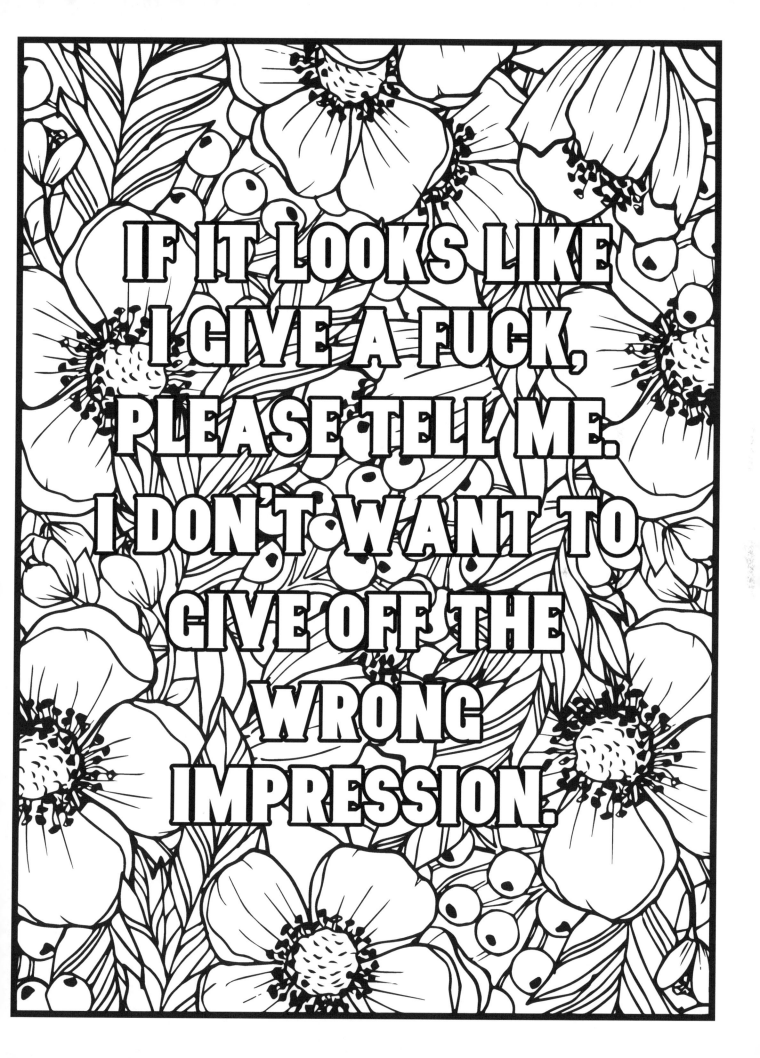

Colorful Swearing Dreams

Swear Word Coloring Book for Adults

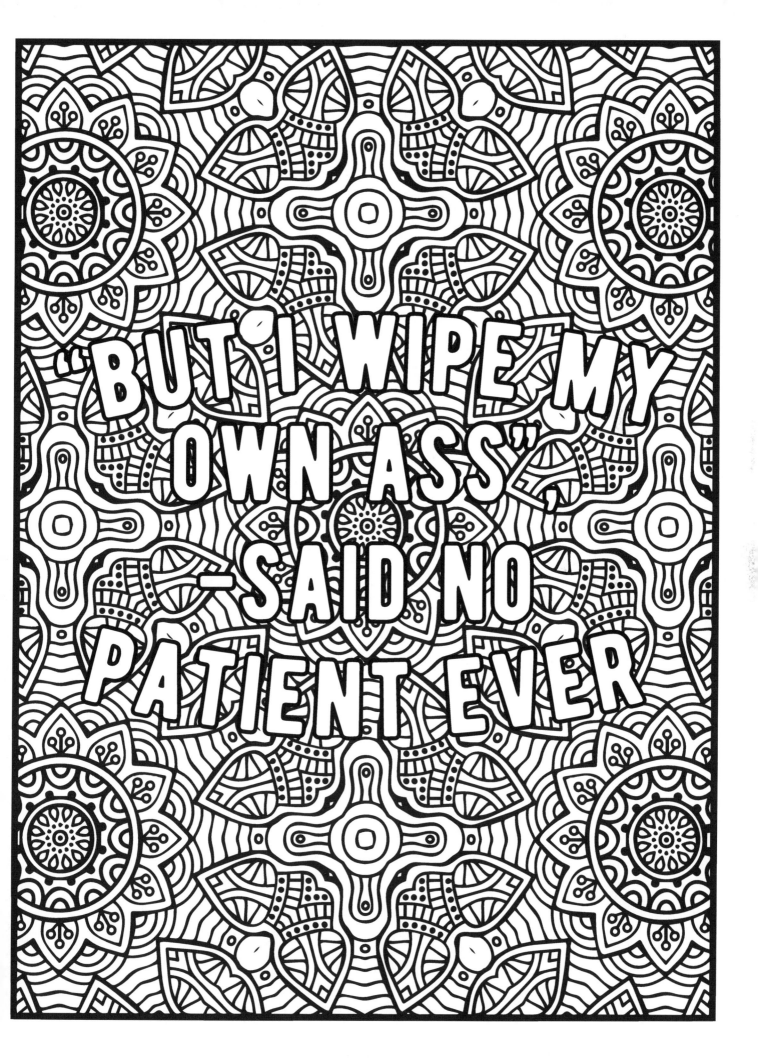

Colorful Swearing Dreams

Swear Word Coloring Book for Adults

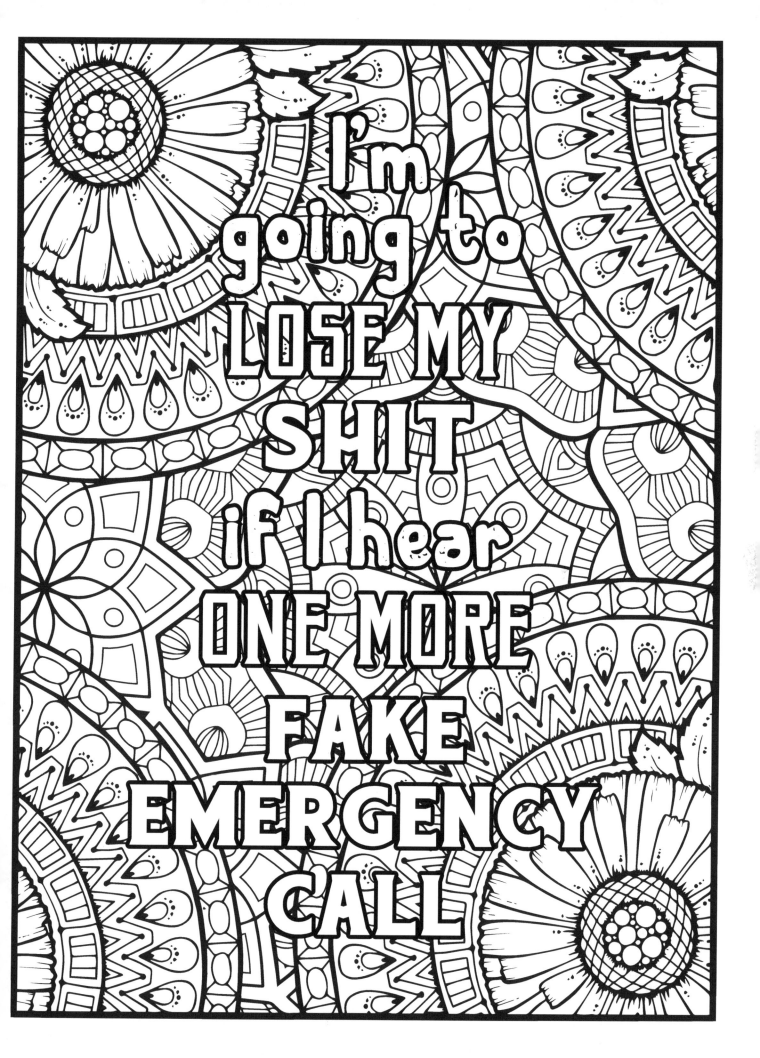

Colorful Swearing Dreams

Swear Word Coloring Book for Adults

Colorful Swearing Dreams

If you liked this book, you'll definitely like our Best Sellers :

(just scan the QR Codes with your Camera app on your phone)

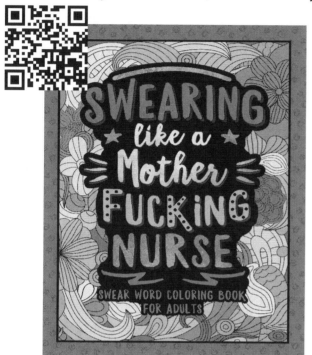

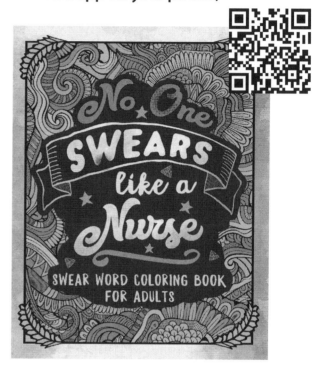

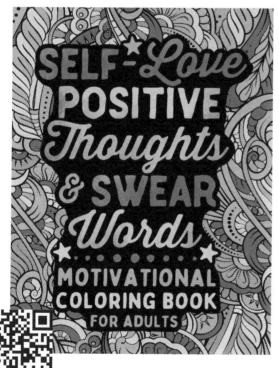

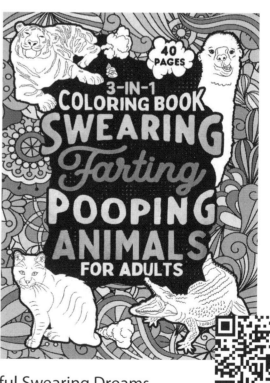

Colorful Swearing Dreams

HOW IS YOUR STRESS LEVEL NOW?

WOULD YOU BE KIND ENOUGH TO REVIEW OUR BOOK?

Did the book allow you to put all the stress out of your mind, body and soul?
Hopefully you now feel fulfilled, relaxed and happy.

YOUR REVIEW is extremely valuable to us.

Your opinion, not only **helps other customers** to make the right decision but
it also allows us to **make other quality products.** The type of gifts that make your friends
and family laugh out loud !

We take pride in making quality products for your satisfaction.

That is why, we would really appreciate if you can take few minutes of your time and
leave us a review on our product's page.

Create Review

 What Nurses Really Want to Say But Can't: Swear Word Coloring Book for Adults with Nursing R...

Overall rating

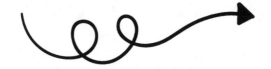

JUST SCAN THE QR CODE WITH THE CAMERA APP ON YOUR PHONE